W9-CBM-029

Biggio
The Final Game

BRIGHT SKY PRESS

2365 Rice Blvd., Suite 202 Houston, Texas 77005

Copyright ©2008 Michael F. Hart

No part of this book may be reproduced in any form or by any electronic or mechanical means, including information storage and
retrieval devices or systems, without prior written permission from the publisher, except that brief passages may be quoted for reviews.

10   9   8   7   6   5   4   3   2   1

Library of Congress Cataloging-in Publication Data

Hart, Michael F., 1949-
Biggio : the final game / by Michael F. Hart.
p. cm.
ISBN 978-1-933979-28-1 (jacketed hardcover : alk. paper) 1. Biggio, Craig. 2. Biggio,
Craig—Portraits. 3. Baseball players—United States. 4. Baseball players—United States—
Portraits. I. Title.

GV865.B53H37 2008
796.357092—dc22

2008018124

Book and cover design by Ellen Peeples Cregan, Cregan Design and Michael Hart
Printed in China through Asia Pacific Offset

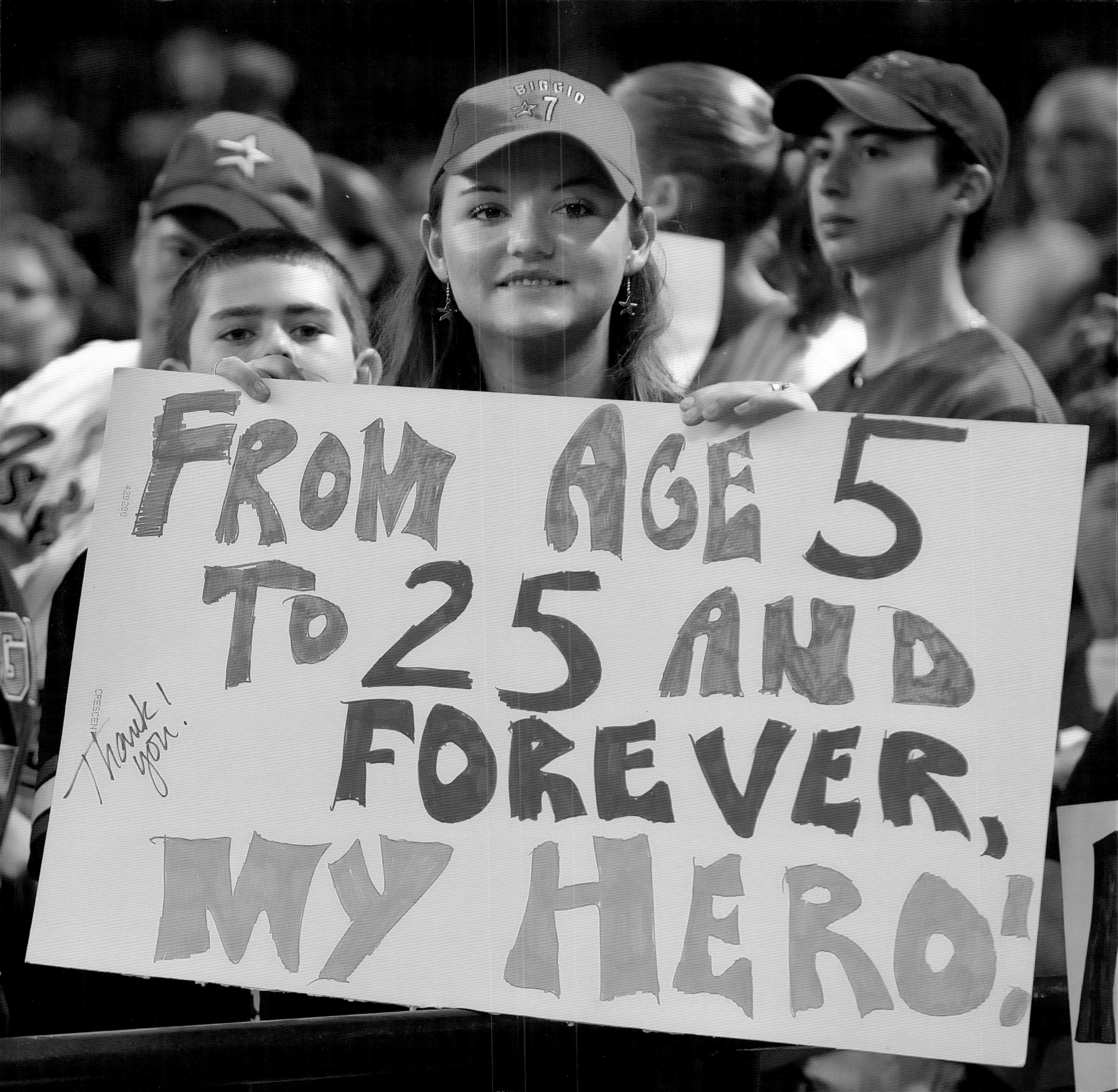
BIGGIO
7
FROM AGE 5
TO 25 AND
FOREVER,
MY HERO!
Thank you!

Craig Biggio's Final Game
Minute Maid Park
Houston, Texas

September 30, 2007

Biggio
The Final Game

PHOTOGRAPHS *by* MICHAEL HART

FOREWORD *by* LARRY DIERKER
AFTERWORD *by* RICHARD JUSTICE

"I am thankful to the fans of Houston,

a city that my family and I have grown to love.

You have treated me and my family with great respect

and affection throughout my career,

and we will forever be appreciative of that."

– CRAIG BIGGIO

FOREWORD *by* LARRY DIERKER

ONE AFTERNOON IN THE SPRING OF 1988, I was standing near the batting cage in Kissimmee, Florida, visiting with Nolan Ryan. The Astros were about to break camp and head for Houston to open the season. Nolan told me that he thought Craig Biggio should make the team despite his lack of experience. I agreed.

What Nolan and I saw was a Hall of Fame player in the making. He had the lightning-quick bat, and he could run from home to first base in less than four seconds, which is extremely rare, especially for a right-handed hitter. And he had the toughness to play catcher, even though he was undersized for the position. Nolan knows only too well that Hall of Fame tools seldom stay sharp long enough to cut a path all the way to Cooperstown. The last five years of any Hall of Fame career are more about desire than ability. To maintain arm strength, foot speed and bat speed, you have to work harder than ever, and this usually happens after you have made all the money you need.

Craig didn't make the team that spring, but he spent only a couple of months at triple-A before he was called to Houston. His enthusiasm was infectious, and his boyish smile captivated Astros fans from the very beginning. His emblematic dirty uniform, torn trousers and the pine tar on his batting helmet are images that any Astros fan can summon in an instant.

Never was the mutual love affair between Craig and the fans more evident than in September of 2007— twenty years after he made it to the majors. Minute Maid Park was packed for nearly every home game in the second half of the 2007 season, even though the Astros were well out of contention. They came out to see the man, and they kept on coming until his last at bat. Those who arrived on time got to see him catch again, which added a little spice to the recipe.

It has always been unusual for a player to play his entire career with one team. But in the high-stakes game of the last twenty years, with free agents fleeing to the highest bidder, and owners shedding salaries to rebuild teams, it is even more unlikely that you will see a Hall of Fame player go wire-to-wire in only one city.

For that to happen, the player often has to take a little less and the owner has to give a little more. Craig Biggio and owner Drayton McLane were able to reach a compromise several times. It would have been easy for Craig to test the market in his prime, and easy for Drayton to let him go when his bat and his legs slowed a bit. But this was not to be. Astros fans will be forever grateful to Biggio for his loyalty and should at least be mindful of McLane's part of the deal.

When Craig got his 3,000th hit on June 28, 2007, the fans went wild. But when he toured the perimeter of Minute Maid Park after his last game, they felt a different kind of emotion—the kind of feeling a parent has when his or her child performs something extraordinary. This was not a time to revel. It was a time to reminisce. It was a joyous occasion, but it was not a time to laugh. Instead, it was a time when a tear might leak out, unexpectedly.

It is my guess that this photo journey of Craig Biggio's last day on the diamond will elicit a few teardrops. And Michael Hart is to be commended for capturing the feelings at Minute Maid that day, and recording them for posterity. These are the first words in this book, and very nearly the last. The message is clear. It needs no words. Simply turn the pages, one by one, and be thankful that you were able to witness something that you will see maybe once in a generation, if you're lucky.

PHOTOGRAPHER'S PREFACE
by MICHAEL HART

THIS BOOK WAS, AND IS, A GIFT.

Let me explain.

My first assignment for the Houston Astros came in September 1989, when their advertising agency enlisted my services for a photographic setup at the Astrodome of three of their rising young players. You will see one of the photographs from that day near the back of the book. Two of those players went on to some prominence, the most heralded being their new starting catcher, a young man from Seton Hall University named Craig Biggio.

Over the next nineteen years I was fortunate to develop an ongoing relationship with the Astros organization. Being a fan as well, I "Stepped Up To The Plate" during their ticket campaign in the late '90's and became a season-ticket holder for several years.

Although the demands of covering a Major League season dictated that the Astros employ a staff photographer, I have continued to do the occasional special project for them, including the yearly team photograph, which, among other uses, becomes a team poster giveaway near the end of each season.

When we shot the 2007 team photo in early September, the city was wrapped up in the conclusion of Craig's now-monumental career. Over 3,000 hits, over 600 doubles (No. 6 on the all-time list, best ever for a right-handed hitter), and all twenty years spent with one team.

I prevailed upon the Astros for a ticket to Craig's last game, but was told that they had been gone for months. My counteroffer was, "Well, let me shoot it for you." Jimmy Stanton, the director of media relations and my client, said, "Sure." So, on September 30, 2007, I found myself in one of the best "seats" in Minute Maid Park. Actually, I was standing the whole time, in the camera pen or on the field before and after the game, but you get the idea.

When I packed my equipment into the car that Sunday morning, I had the thought that I should go back in the house and get a handkerchief. I frequently describe myself as a sentimentalist, and that was certainly the case that day. Along with 43,000 fans in the stands, I found myself caught up in the intense emotions of the day.

As Craig was leaving the dugout to take the field at the top of the sixth inning, he motioned to me, and when I leaned over he said, "Tell everyone I want to get some of these photos." A reasonable request, given the historic significance of the day, the swan song for a future Hall of Fame player.

When I started examining the 800-plus images I shot that day, I really liked what I saw, and thought, heck, instead of just doing up a few random prints, or a disc of images, I would try one of the high-level book services I had been wanting to test out.

So I put together eighty pages of photographs and had three copies made: one for Craig, one for myself, and one for my assignment rep, Melody George, to share with our clients and potential clients.

The response we received was amazing. Men, as well as women, would start tearing up while looking at the images. Some had been at the game and remembered specific moments. Others wished they had, and replayed the events of that day vicariously. Above all, we felt the admiration that so many had for this man. A man who played the game with intensity and passion, but also with respect. A man who stayed true to the city which embraced him, eschewing undoubtedly more money had he moved on to more lucrative offers when contracts were up. Above all, a devoted family man in a day when so many of our "heroes" end up having feet of clay, and less than stellar values. Indeed, my favorite image in the book is the one of Craig and one of his sons, watching the final inning from the dugout, their heads resting against each other.

We started thinking about the possibility of sharing this with a larger audience, and through a number of small miracles, that has indeed come to pass. And it became a larger vision with the participation of Larry Dierker and Richard Justice, an old and a new friend, respectively, who have put into words much more eloquently than I ever could the impact on Houston and the game of baseball that Craig Biggio's career has left.

So, as I said in the beginning, this book was, and is, a gift; first to Craig and Patty and their family; and then to me, my family and friends; and, ultimately, I hope, to you.

September 30, 2007, was an incredibly emotional experience for a baseball fan, especially a fan of the Houston Astros and Craig Biggio. I hope you get the sense of that in these pages.

PREGAME

I HAD SECURED A PHOTO PASS to what everyone knew was going to be one of baseball's historic games. As I packed my camera gear into the car on September 30, 2007, to go photograph the Astros taking on the Braves, I realized that this was not only going to be one for the books, it would be a real tearjerker, too. Since I'm the sentimental type, I went back for a handkerchief. I should have brought two.

There's always great energy before a major league game, but everyone knew this was a once-in-a-lifetime event. Craig Biggio's final game ended one of the most impressive runs of any modern baseball player. Twenty years, wire-to-wire, Craig played for the Astros. Not only is this kind of dedication rare in any industry these days, but also, within those twenty years, he became Houston's most beloved sports icon. It's not just his stats—his 3,060 hits, his 668 doubles, or his almost 300 homers, all impressive in their own right—it's that Craig is a real sports hero: women love him, little boys want to be him, and fathers admire him. And that afternoon, everyone wanted to honor him.

By ten in the morning, the crowd looped around the block for a game that wouldn't start until 1:30. Everyone was going nuts. The Astros' people commented that it was crazier than the World Series had been. The anticipation was thicker than the mustard on the hot dogs; this crowd knew it was part of baseball history.

I slipped through the lines into the press door and took my place in the camera pen at the far end of the first-base dugout. When I got settled, I realized that not only did I have a perfect view of the game, I had a perfect view of the man, as Craig and his two sons chose to sit by themselves at the far end of the dugout, within feet of my lens. I also had a straight shot towards second base for any double plays that Craig might turn.

Talking to a cop before the game, I commented that I was glad I had gone back for that handkerchief. He nodded and silently showed me his. Other players continued autographing, but as time for the first pitch drew near, Craig went off quietly with his family. Their sense of togetherness was strong. This game, as Craig's career had been, was a real family deal.

The National Anthem struck up, and as I felt the normal chill from hearing that tune at the ball game, I saw Craig's wife Patty tearing up. I knew just how she felt. All 43,823 fans in Minute Maid Park, a record crowd, were sharing a very emotional moment with the Biggios.

At the last strains of the anthem, the fans started screaming. Their faces transformed, as if they were seeing a legendary rock star. Drayton McLane introduced Craig, and gave him a framed second base, tagged to commemorate the day, surrounded by his baseball cards and pictures of all the Astros' uniforms he had worn—including some of the more dubious ones. He read a letter to Craig from Bud Selig, the baseball commissioner: "I look forward to our paths crossing in the very near future and again, several years from now, in Cooperstown." Most fittingly, the Astros' owner also gave him a check for the Sunshine Kids, the charity Craig has supported so well: $3,059.00—one dollar for each career hit to that point.

Craig and his daughter, Quinn, threw out the first pitch to his sons, Cavan and Conor, and it was "Play ball!" Lucky Number 7 took the field for the final time.

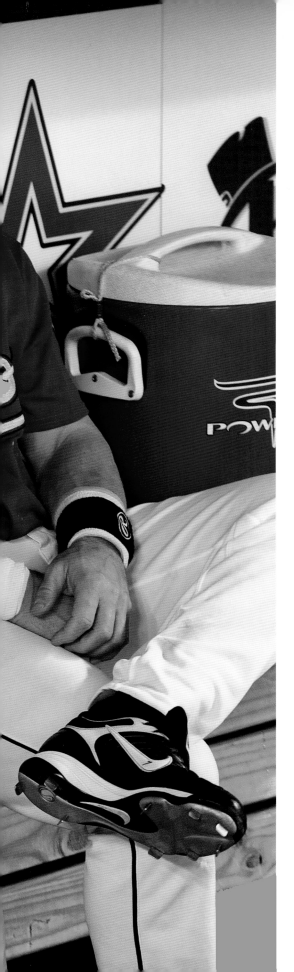

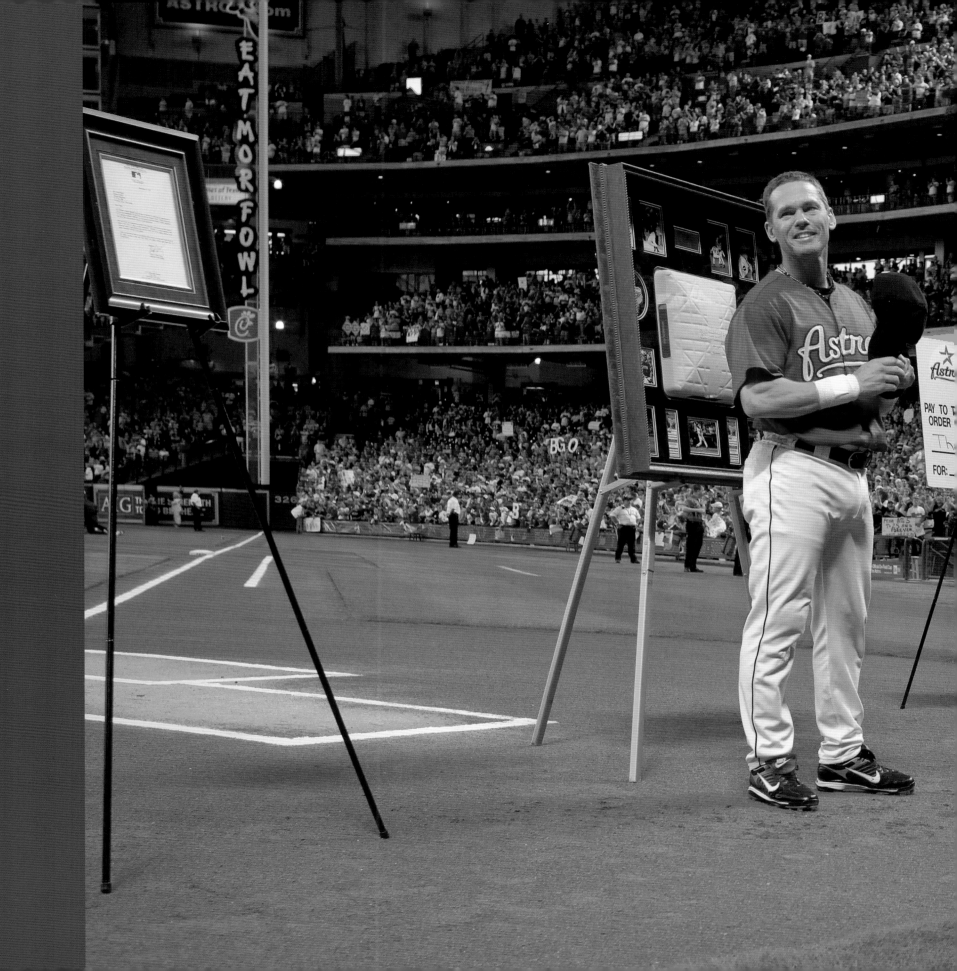

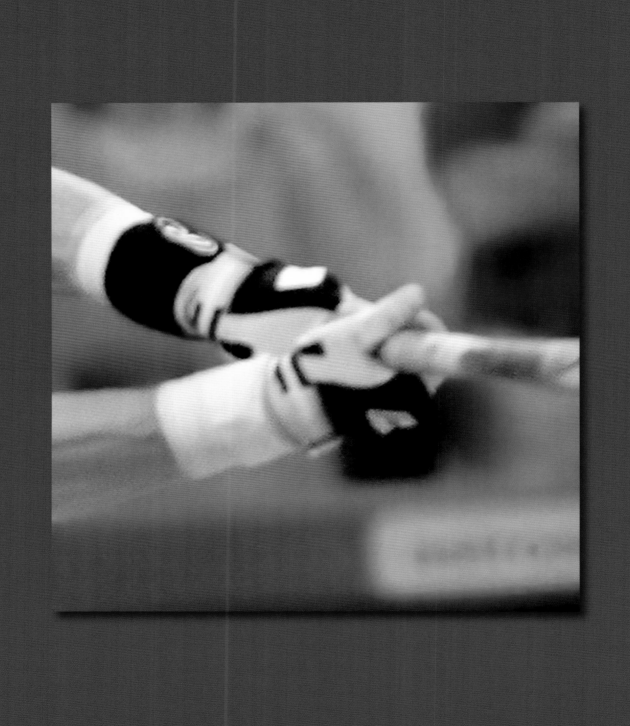

THE FINAL HIT

WHEN A BATTER WITH OVER THREE THOUSAND HITS goes to the plate, the crowd leans forward, waiting. This afternoon, as Craig headed up the steps and stepped on deck, no one bothered with the edge of the seat. The tension pulled them to their feet as a unit. Craig tipped his hat to their standing ovation. Camera flashes popped all over the stadium, so many in fact, that later, as I perused the images on my computer, I realized they made a blue haze that I had to tone down, as if the energy was visible.

What would he do? He stepped up to the plate. Fittingly for the top right-handed doubles hitter of all time, Craig smashed a double. It was hit number 3,060.

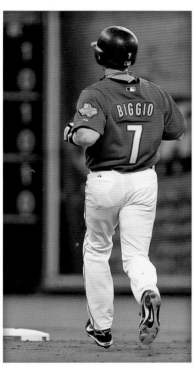

THE FINAL RUN

AFTER CRAIG'S DOUBLE PUT HIM ON BASE, Carlos Lee knocked him in on a single. Craig met his teammates' rush to greet him at the dugout steps with a big old grin. As Craig ran it in, I even spied Braves manager Bobby Cox clapping for him. For this play, it wasn't about the competition; it was about the game itself, and the man who represented it so honorably.

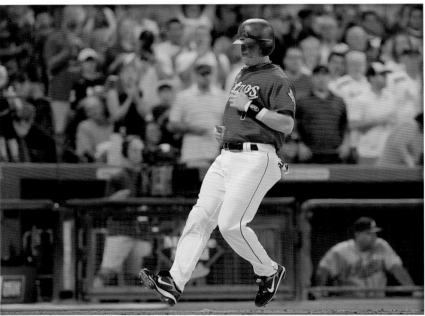

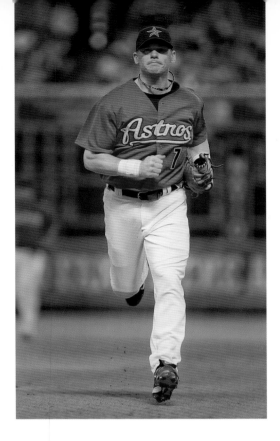

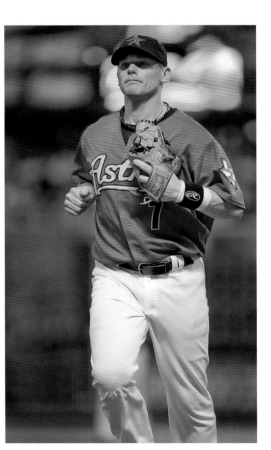

THE DOUBLE PLAY

FROM MY VANTAGE POINT IN THE CAMERA PEN, I knew I had a great line on second base. Anytime Atlanta got a man on first, I pre-focused on second, waiting to catch Craig finishing off one of his trademark double plays. It's the ultimate second baseman's play, and it's risky. The runners are always trying to take the defense out. I knew that Craig's only real injury during his career was the result of a double play. But this afternoon, it snapped like clockwork. The intensity so emblematic of Craig's play is evident in his face as he tags the bag ahead of Scott Thorman's slide and follows the flight of his throw right into Lance Berkman's glove.

Between innings we saw video tributes from each of the Biggio children. Each piece conveyed the love these kids have for their Dad, but the last one, which was played in the middle of the seventh, from his daughter, Quinn, reminded us all that Craig is as fine a father as he is a ballplayer. When her little voice rang out, "I love you, Daddy," it seemed as if I could see straight into Craig's heart. Without my camera, I would have felt intrusive watching this giant of the diamond listen to "Take Me Out to the Ball Game" for the last time in uniform. We love you, too, Craig.

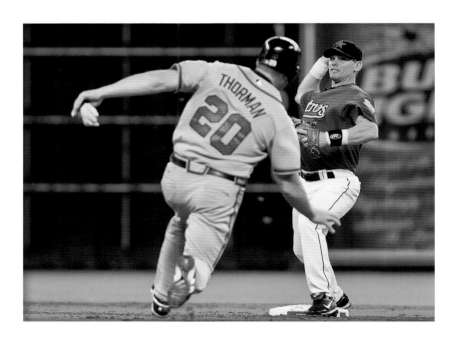

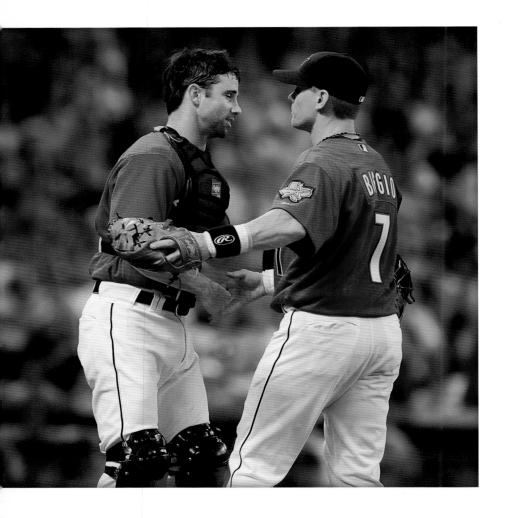

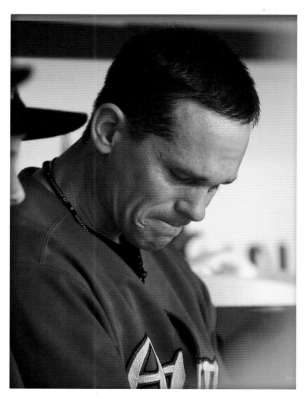

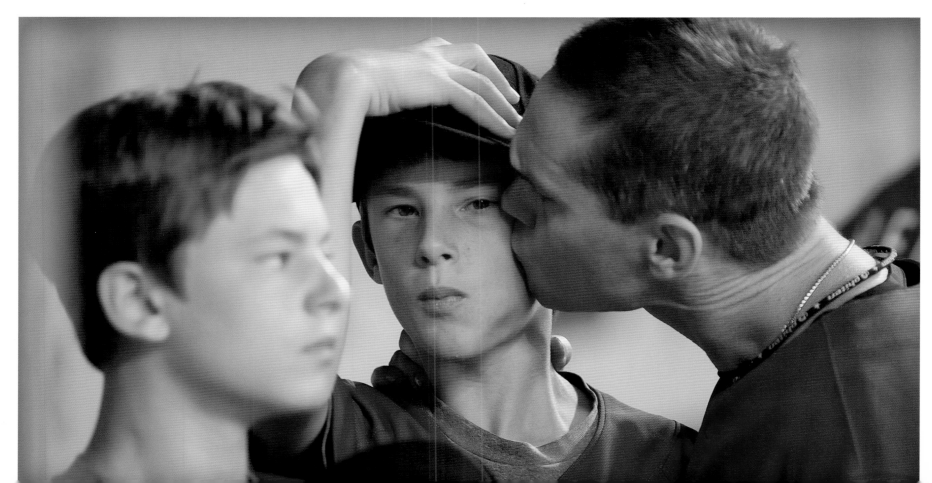

THE FINAL AT BAT

CRAIG'S FACE MADE IT OBVIOUS how aware he was that this was his last at bat. Cecil Cooper had been subbing out the other starters, and the time for the carefully thought-out exit that had been in the forefront of our minds all season had come. It was to be a grand exit. As the crowd erupted in yet another powerful standing ovation, Craig stood with his head down. The intensity of the moment vibrated from the plate up through the cheap seats. Craig said something to the ump and tapped him with his bat. They were down in the score, but Bobby Cox's Braves were a class act. Magnanimously, they let Craig have his moment. They knew this display of affection and respect for Craig was bigger than one game. Ron Mahay, their pitcher, grabbed the rosin bag and stepped off the mound, giving Craig as much time as he needed before tossing out the last pitches he would swing for. Craig grounded out to Chipper Jones at third base. Jones took as long as I've ever seen a third baseman take to return the ball to first base. After the game, he said that all he thought as he threw the out was "Run, Craig, run." The measure of a man is often clearest in his opponents' eyes.

Craig must have felt the respect of his opponents, because as he left the field, he tipped his hat to the Braves' dugout.

FAREWELL

AT THE START OF THE EIGHTH INNING, ATLANTA WAS UP. Before anyone was at bat, Houston called time, and Craig left the field as manager Cecil Cooper sent in Cody Ransom to replace him. Although Craig was tight-lipped, the emotion was rampant on his face. The fans' ovation roared, lasting over five minutes. Before Craig returned to the dugout, he hugged the Braves' first-base coach. Through all of it, the Braves' batter stood back, politely. It was the Astros' show, it was Houston's show, and mostly it was Craig Biggio's show. Graciously, he acknowledged the crowd all around him, the people who loved him, whose respect he worked so hard to earn and keep. For twenty years, he had been all business on the field, always methodical, always determined, and this afternoon we saw not only his incredible work ethic, but also the passion for the game that fueled it.

As the game wound down, Craig watched the final Astros and Braves at-bats with his arms around his boys in the dugout.

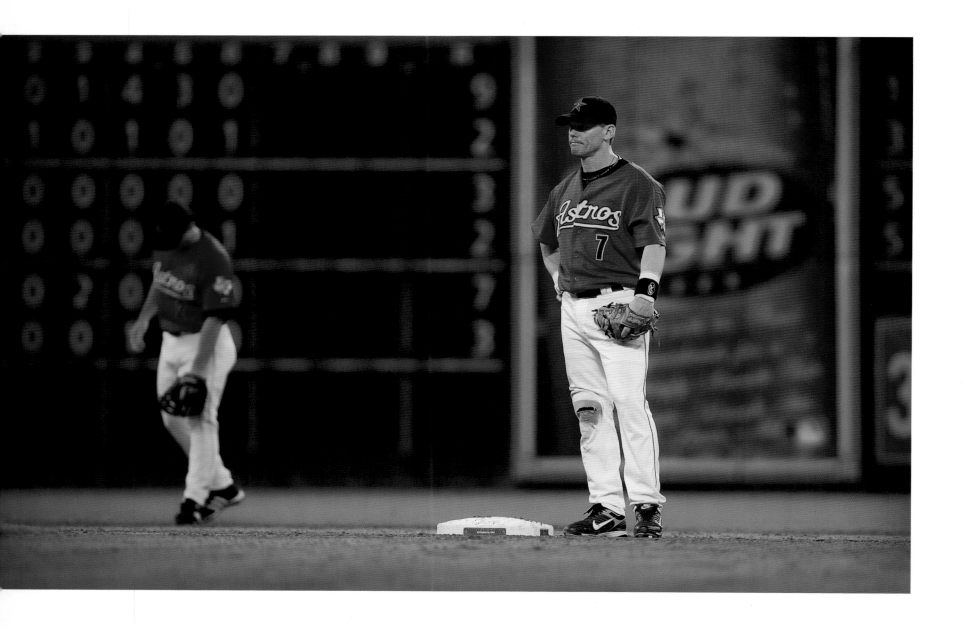

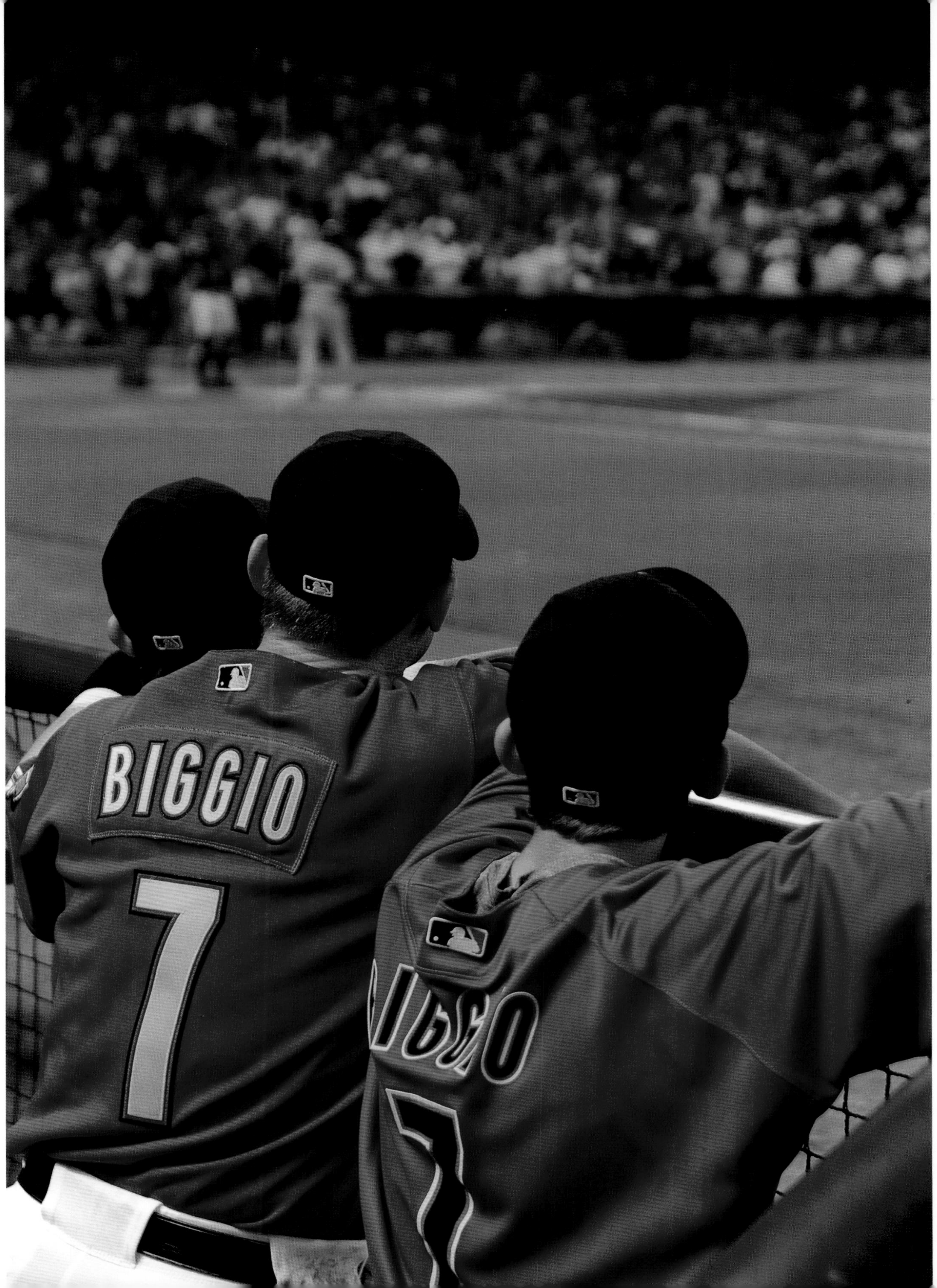
BIGGIO
7

POSTGAME

THEN IT WAS OVER. As the victorious Astros headed to the field to shake hands after the game, Craig hung back. He and Jeff Bagwell had made an agreement that once they left the game, they would remain outside of the diamond. Craig took a trip around the perimeter of the field, waving to the fans. Spontaneously, he broke into a trot, and everyone started following him. There were handslaps, and well-wishes, and already nostalgia was setting in. When we looked up from watching our star take his last lap, the Braves were gone. They had quietly faded off the field to leave these waning moments to the Astros' family: the players, their wives and children; the press who had followed Biggio from catcher, to second base, to center field and back to second; the thousands of fans of every age in their # 7 jerseys—everyone who had rooted for Craig and his one team, the Houston Astros, for so long.

Craig Biggio will not return to the diamond. Even outside the lines, he will never leave our hearts, no matter how many other boys of summer may come after him. Unless his great friend Jeff Bagwell beats him to Cooperstown, when Craig is elected to the Hall of Fame, it will be the first time that a player will enter in an Astros uniform. How fitting that it will be the ripped uniform and the pine-tar-stained helmet of this man who left it all on the field.

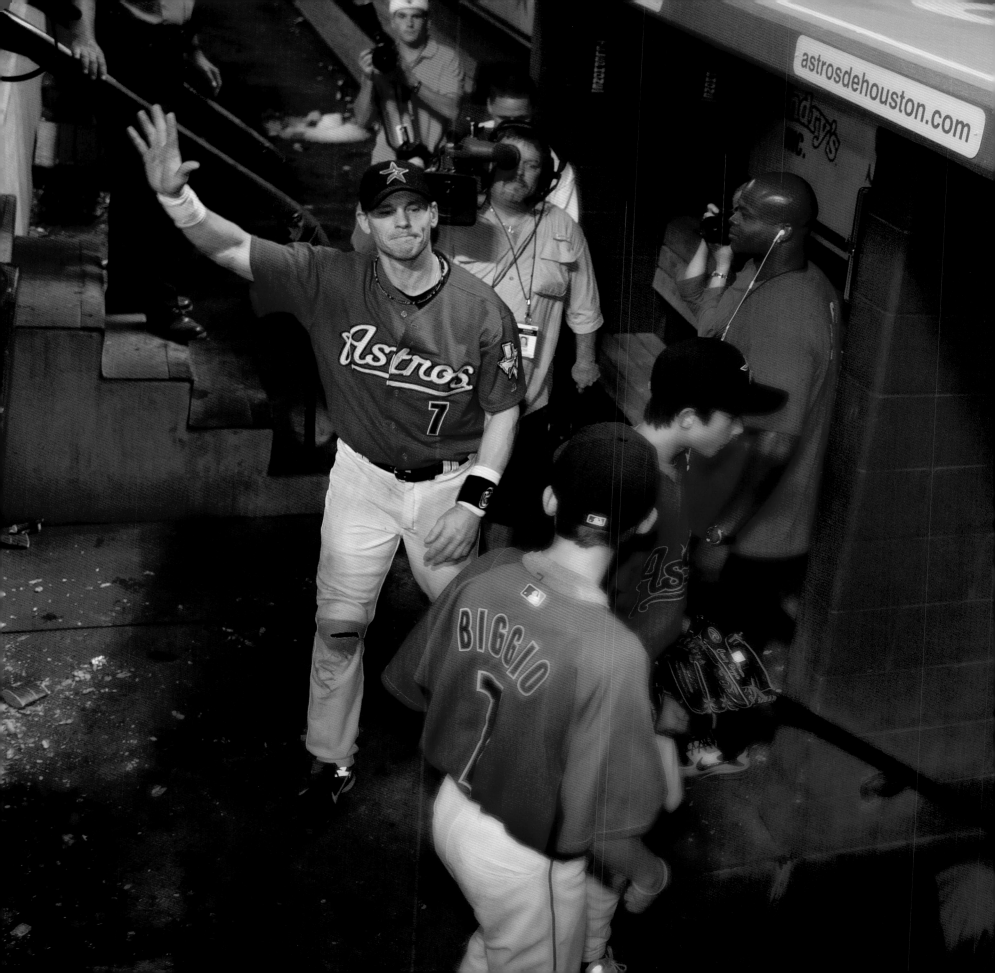

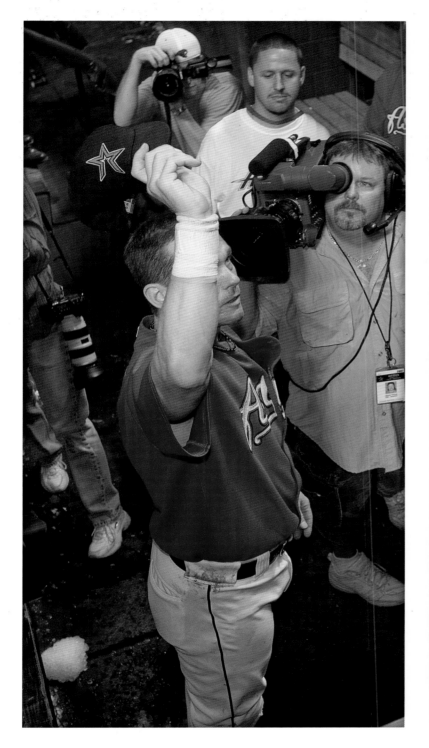 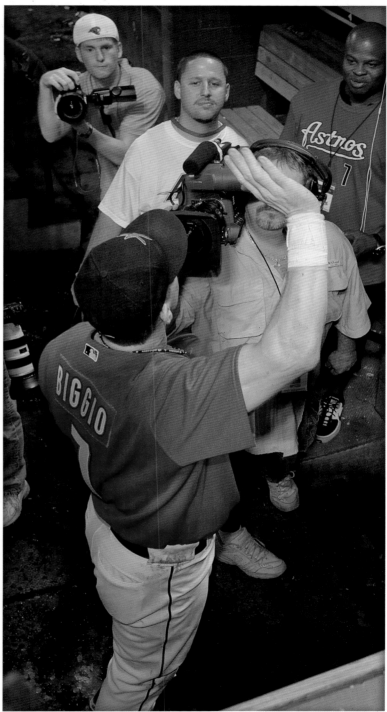

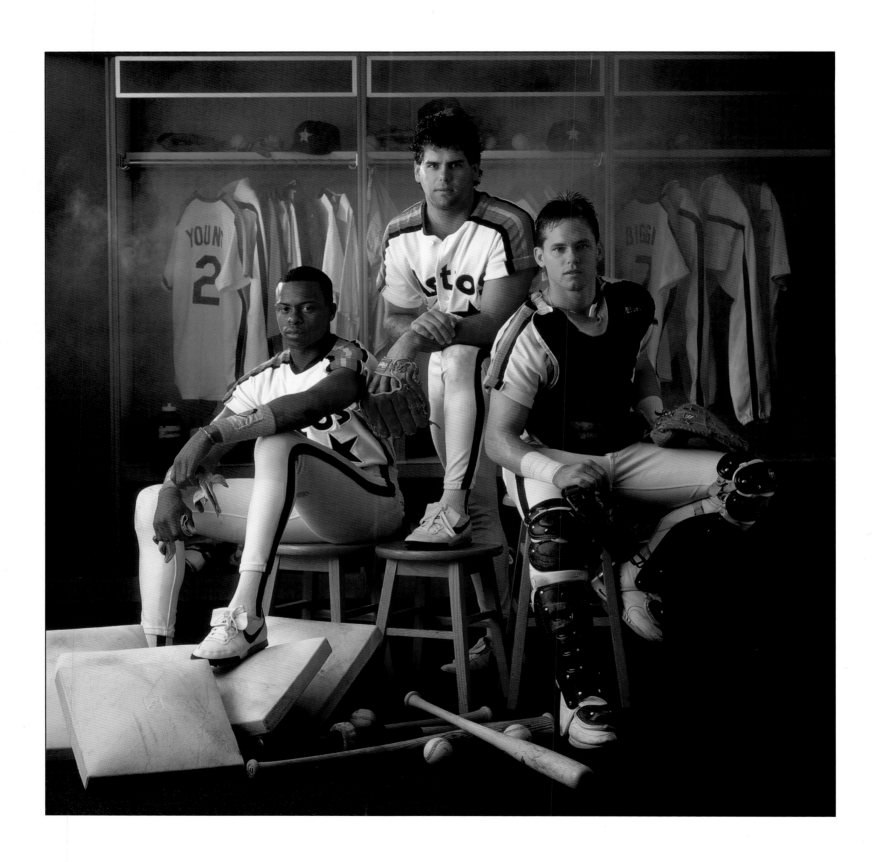

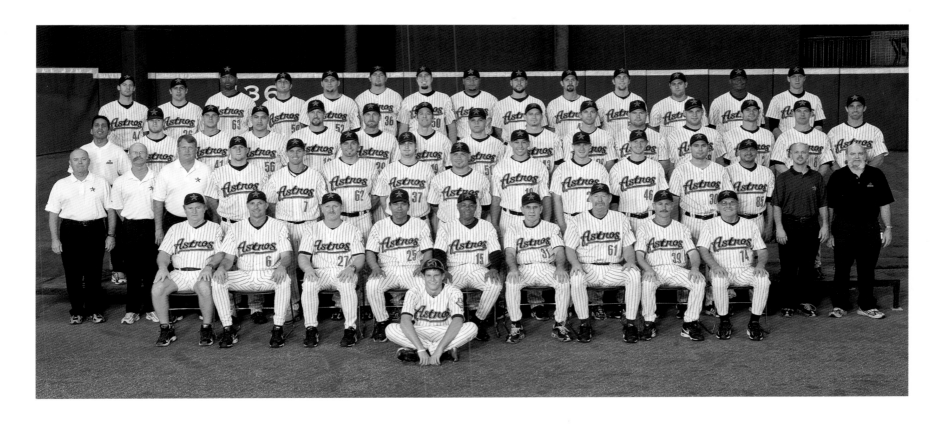

From the first photograph, in an Astrodome locker room in 1989,
to the last team photo in September 2007, I have been a fan as well as a photographer.

Recording the events of September 30, 2007 was an emotional experience that I will never forget,
and I feel honored to be able to provide you with a memento of that special day.

Michael Hart
Houston, Texas

AFTERWORD *by* RICHARD JUSTICE

LET'S GO INSIDE THE HOME CLUBHOUSE AT MINUTE MAID PARK to the locker that's halfway down the row on the right, just behind the sofas and facing the big-screen television. For the last eight seasons, it belonged to Craig Biggio.

Biggio wept the day he boxed up the family pictures and fan letters, the bobble-heads and T-shirts and all the other stuff he'd collected through the years. That locker had been his and his alone, as comfortable as a pair of shoes.

Lance Berkman now occupies it, and if that seems cold, that's the way these things work in sports. Besides, the team that was once run by Biggio and his buddy, Jeff Bagwell, is now Berkman's, at least in terms of seniority.

In ways large and small, the Astros will always belong to Biggio and Bagwell, two players that helped transform a losing, nondescript franchise into one of baseball's most successful. The 2007 season was the final part of the journey. Bagwell played his last game in 2005, so 2007 belonged to Biggio.

There's no good way to end these things. Not after twenty seasons. Not after all the memories, especially not for a player that established himself as one of the best ever.

His 3,060 hits were the twentieth-most in the century or so that there has been major league baseball. That last summer had been a humbling experience as Biggio climbed the all-time list, passing Hall of Famers like Roberto Clemente and Al Kaline, cementing a legacy of accomplishment that will take him through the doors of the Hall of Fame in 2013.

For the people of Houston, he was more than just a great ballplayer. He was the Jersey boy that settled here, raised a family, and became part of the community.

He'd attempted to soak it all in during that last season, to try and remember. There was the last trip to Dodger Stadium, the last one to Milwaukee, etc. In the hours before each game, hours when baseball players sometimes play cards or watch television, he'd take a long look around the rooms and the hallways, the bat racks, the scoreboards.

This had been his life. Packed houses. A kid's game. Yes, he'd been lucky.

At Minute Maid Park, he had some of the best and worst days of his life. There was the time he attempted to play a game after learning one of his buddies and former teammates, Daryl Kile, had died. There were playoff defeats and playoff victories and countless nights when small heroics seemed like big things.

Inside the clubhouse, though, that's the place where relationships are forged and teams built. A baseball clubhouse is a special place. It's the private sanctuary of the players. For five months each season, the clubhouse is where players spend almost as much time as they spend at home.

The Astros have a large one with carpeting and big comfortable chairs and photographs. There's usually a pot of soup simmering in the back, except on Sunday morning when a guy makes BLTs that have become as much a part of the club's traditions as exploding scoreboards.

You can learn a lot about a player by looking at his locker. Virtually all of them have family photos. Berkman keeps his boots there. One year he posted a sign indicating he'd talked enough about (a) his knee and (b) steroids. Brad Ausmus got so annoyed by Bagwell's victory cigars that he attached a dozen small fans to his locker.

Biggio's locker was almost in the middle of the room. Ausmus had the space on the right, Hunter Pence on the left. For years, Biggio and Bagwell dressed, ate, laughed and occasionally cried beside one another. As Drayton McLane told us dozens of times, they were the heart and soul of the Houston Astros.

Biggio, now the old guy, attempted to make the transition from teammate to mentor that final season. Hunter Pence became his guy.

Pence watched Biggio closely. He asked question after question and made it clear he wanted to be like Biggio. For the managers and coaches, this was a good sign that Pence understood that the way to make it in baseball was to care as much as Biggio cared, to be as meticulous in his preparation and as serious about his approach as Biggio.

The thing that's so remarkable about Biggio's twenty seasons was that he remained pretty much the same every day. He broke records and won games and did things few players had ever done. Yet, he never changed much. His life was built around conditioning drills, batting practice, meals and family. He was so focused on doing things the right way that he joked that he was boring.

Since we're in the clubhouse, let's rewind one year and check out his game bats. Yes, it's those four laid on the carpet in front of his locker. Don't touch, just look. He has them just the way he likes them.

Biggio spent part of almost every day sanding, taping and smearing those bats with pine tar. He would swing the bats and sand some more and swing again. When he got the bat just right, he would lay it in front of his locker, just so.

Speaking of his locker, he was fussy about it. He wanted everything in a certain place and was so organized he could be blindfolded and still find his gloves, sunglasses or hat.

His pre-game routine spoke volumes about how he approached his job. Other players were more talented. Other players were bigger, stronger or faster. But no player ever cared more or got more from his physical skills.

He always tried to do the right thing, and perhaps that's why Craig Biggio's legacy is so simple. He didn't just talk the talk. He embraced the fact that he was a role model, that old and young alike would be using him as an example.

That's why he was so careful with everything he did, from his wardrobe to his speech to the way he played the game. He understood that people were paying attention.

If he failed to run out a ground ball, cursed an umpire or embarrassed a teammate, he knew that kids all over Houston would think it was acceptable for them to do the same thing.

Maybe that's why we loved him so much, and maybe that's why his final season with the Astros was so special. We knew there'd never be another like him.

He was not a reflective or sentimental person by nature, but in 2007, at the end of a twenty-year career that had included playoff appearances and an encyclopedia of highs and lows, he occasionally forced himself to look back.

He'd also occasionally look around the stands at Minute Maid Park. It was as if he was trying to soak it all in, to have a clear memory long after the cheers had stopped.

He was constantly struck by all those people wearing jerseys with his number 7. Not just kids, but older men and middle-aged women and college students.

These were people that might not have agreed on a single thing in everyday life. They simply agreed that they loved Craig Biggio, that they appreciated his sense of responsibility and the fact that he was a man of faith and dignity.

Through the years, they approached him at stores and in restaurants to simply shake his hand and tell him thanks for representing Houston so well. In that final season, though, it hit him hard at times that, yes, he'd made a difference.

Between the time Biggio arrived in the big leagues in 1988 and the afternoon he left in 2007, the Astros became one of baseball's most successful franchises. Not just successful, but respected. They did things with class.

During Biggio's career, we shared one sweet moment after another as our little hardball team went to the playoffs six times in nine seasons, including those magical runs of 2004 and 2005. That night in 2005 when the Astros went to St. Louis and clinched their first National League pennant, when they finally brought the World Series to Texas, there was a feeling of accomplishment almost beyond words.

Tucked into the corner of the locker room, saying little, struggling for the right word, mostly just soaking it all in, sat Biggio. Hours later, he was still there, tired and happy and emotional.

During that final season, we unashamedly shed tears the night Biggio became the twentieth player in more than a century of big league baseball to collect 3,000 hits.

That was also the night we began saying our goodbyes to Craig Biggio. Even before he announced that the 2007 season would be his last, we sensed his time was almost up.

He cried some in those final weeks, as he remembered how quickly it had all gone. He remembered veterans like Alan Ashby and Billy Doran, who took him under their wings even though they understood he was being groomed to take their jobs.

Doran flew to Houston one winter to help Biggio make the transition from catcher to second base. Doran knew his time as an everyday player was over, but for a week, he took Biggio into the Astrodome, walked off an infield in the rodeo dirt and taught him the finer points of second base.

Biggio choked back tears one day as he remembered Ken Caminiti. They'd once been the best of friends, but through the years as Caminiti fought—and ultimately lost—his fight against addiction, they grew apart.

A few weeks before the 2007 season, Biggio moved Caminiti's body from its original burial place to his South Texas ranch. With permission of the Caminiti family Biggio found just the right spot for his tortured friend, laid him to rest once and for all and said a prayer.

By the time he played that final game, Biggio had made Houston his home in almost every sense of the word. His kids were born in Houston, many of his friends were there and he'd done more than be a great player. He'd been a great citizen, too. His work with the Sunshine Kids was from the heart.

He left us all with countless memories of average nights made extraordinary by Craig Biggio. Perhaps there was a time when he simply was another ballplayer. By that final season, though, he was much more than that.

When it was all over, Biggio said something about being lucky. He's wrong about that. We're the lucky ones.

Biggio: The Final Game has been selected for inclusion in the Library of the Baseball Hall of Fame, Cooperstown, New York.

ACKNOWLEDGEMENTS

I WOULD LIKE TO THANK A NUMBER OF PEOPLE who in one way or another have made this book possible. Jimmy Stanton, Astros' director of media relations, who is my client for the yearly team photo, made it possible for me to be in the position I was in on September 30. His former media manager, Charlie Hepp, who has since "defected" to the Colorado Rockies, assigned me the prime spot in the far first-base pen that made many of the shots possible.

In addition, my many contacts at the Astros over the years have made doing assignments for them fun, from Norm Miller on that initial shoot in 1989, to the many years I spent working with Rob Matwick (now with the Detroit Tigers), who became a good friend, to the current group, including Pam Gardner, Jaimie Hildreth, Jay Lucas, Rita Suchma, Sally Gunter, John Sorrentino and, of course, Drayton McLane.

Special thanks for encouragement in getting the project off the ground go to my office neighbor, Peter Cook of Whittenton Industries, whose enthusiasm for the project was palpable; my former FPG Stock Photo editor Paul Cunningham, now with Major League Baseball Properties in New York; Rich Lord of SportsRadio 610; David Gow of 1560 AM The Game, who graciously made the introduction to Richard Justice; my good friend of over 30 years, Richard Ethun; and of course my longtime assignments representative, Melody George, who started telling me stories of our commercial clients' enthusiasm for the initial book that she showed them. I am also indebted to Larry Dierker and Richard Justice for joining us without hesitation; their views of Craig from two "insider's positions" give us all a glimpse into his professional and personal career that is truly a gift.

And of course my friend and client, Ellen Peeples Cregan, and her colleagues at Bright Sky Press—Rue Judd, Lucy Chambers, and Leslie Little—made the actual publication a reality.

In the preface, I mentioned a number of small miracles happening to make this book a reality. Probably the biggest of those began when my friend John Brejot of CBS Radio in Houston, put me back in touch with another contact from past days with the Astros. Alicia Nevins has not only handled the contact with Craig and his agent, Barry Axelrod, but has been instrumental in drumming up support for the book. She was solely responsible for getting it reviewed by and accepted into the Baseball Hall of Fame in Cooperstown, NY. Without her enthusiasm and encouragement, this project simply would not have happened, and she receives my eternal gratitude.

The images in this book were made utilizing Canon cameras and lenses. The majority of exposures were made on a Canon 1Ds Mark II; a few were done on a Canon 1Ds. The lenses utilized were a 300mm f2.8L; a 28-70 f2.8L, and a 70-200 f2.8L. The RAW files were imported onto an Apple MacPro workstation and converted to Adobe Digital Negatives.

All files were processed in Adobe Camera Raw, utilizing the ProPhoto Color Space in 16-bit, and optimized in Adobe Photoshop on an Eizo CG211 monitor. Nik Dfine 2.0 was employed for noise reduction. The final files were converted into Adobe 1998 at 8-bit, output sharpened with PixelGenius PhotoKit sharpener, and finally converted to CMYK for the offset press.

HFLOW 796
.3570
92
H326

HART, MICHAEL F.
  BIGGIO

FLORES
10/08